AF228175

EXPLORING NATURE

Spotting Birds

BY LAURA PERDEW

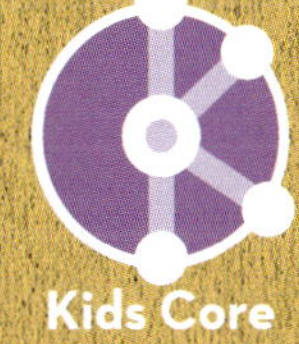

Kids Core
An Imprint of Abdo Publishing
abdobooks.com

abdobooks.com

Published by Abdo Publishing, a division of ABDO, PO Box 398166, Minneapolis, Minnesota 55439. Copyright © 2026 by Abdo Consulting Group, Inc. International copyrights reserved in all countries. No part of this book may be reproduced in any form without written permission from the publisher. Kids Core™ is a trademark and logo of Abdo Publishing.

Printed in the United States of America, North Mankato, Minnesota.
102025
012026

Cover Photo: Brian A. Wolf/Shutterstock Images
Interior Photos: Anatoliy Lukich/Shutterstock Images, 4–5; Lane Oatey/Blue Jean Images/Getty Images, 7; Harry Collins Photography/Shutterstock Images, 8; damircudic/E+/Getty Images, 10–11; Shutterstock Images, 13, 18, 23, 28 (bottom left), 28 (bottom right); Richard G. Smith/Shutterstock Images, 14; Annette Shaff/Shutterstock Images, 15; Aoy Charin/Shutterstock Images, 17; Jim Cumming/Shutterstock Images, 20–21; Melody Mellinger/Shutterstock Images, 24; iStockphoto, 26; Peter Titmuss/Alamy, 28 (top); Anastasiia Yurevych/Shutterstock Images, 29

Editor: Marie Pearson
Series Designer: Marley Richmond

Library of Congress Control Number: 2025939878

Publisher's Cataloging-in-Publication Data

Names: Perdew, Laura, author.
Title: Spotting birds / by Laura Perdew
Description: Minneapolis, Minnesota: Abdo Publishing, 2026 | Series: Exploring nature | Includes online resources and index.
Identifiers: ISBN 9781098298708 (lib. bdg.) | ISBN 9798384932505 (ebook)
Subjects: LCSH: Bird watching--Juvenile literature. | Birds--behavior--Juvenile literature. | Zoology--Juvenile literature. | Nature--Juvenile literature. | Ecological science--Juvenile literature. | Habitats (Ecology)--Juvenile literature.
Classification: DDC 598.072--dc23

CONTENTS

CHAPTER 1

What's That Bird? 4

CHAPTER 2

Looking for Birds 10

CHAPTER 3

Identifying Birds 20

Field Notes 28
Glossary 30
Online Resources 31
Learn More 31
Index 32
About the Author 32

Steller's jays can be spotted in the western United States.

What's That Bird?

Marwa and her grandmother sit at a picnic table eating lunch. When they finish, they will go bird-watching. Nearby, a chickadee calls, *chickadee-dee-dee*. And then a bird lands right on their table!

Grandma hands Marwa the bird guide so she can identify their visitor. The bird's wing feathers are mostly blue, and it has a black head with a crest. Its black beak is long and slightly curved. And the bird is loud! Marwa declares, "It's a Steller's jay!"

What Is a Bird?

The Steller's jay is one of more than 11,000 species of birds on Earth. Birds live on every

Not All Birds Fly

Not all birds can fly. There are about 60 species of flightless birds. Flightless birds have other abilities. Penguins can dive deep underwater to find food. Ostriches have strong legs. They can run fast and kick hard.

continent, including Antarctica. They survive in every type of **habitat**, including wetlands, forests, deserts, grasslands, tundra, and water. They can even live in **urban** areas. A scientist who studies birds and their habitats is called an ornithologist. People who regularly look for birds are called birders.

Barred owls are a type of raptor. People can sometimes spot them during the day, though the birds are most active at night.

All birds have feathers and two wings. Birds that fly have strong, hollow bones. The spaces inside the bones allow a bird to breathe in more oxygen during flight. All birds reproduce by laying eggs. All birds also have two legs.

Birds use their feet to walk, perch, swim, or waddle. Water birds have webbed feet that let them paddle in water. **Raptors** use sharp **talons** on their feet to hunt.

People can spot birds just about anywhere. Bird-watching is a great way to connect with nature. It does not cost much. And birding can be done alone or shared with family and friends.

Further Evidence

Look at the website below. Does it give any new evidence to support Chapter One?

What Makes a Bird . . . a Bird?

abdocorelibrary.com/spotting-birds

People may be able to see
and hear birds as they fly.

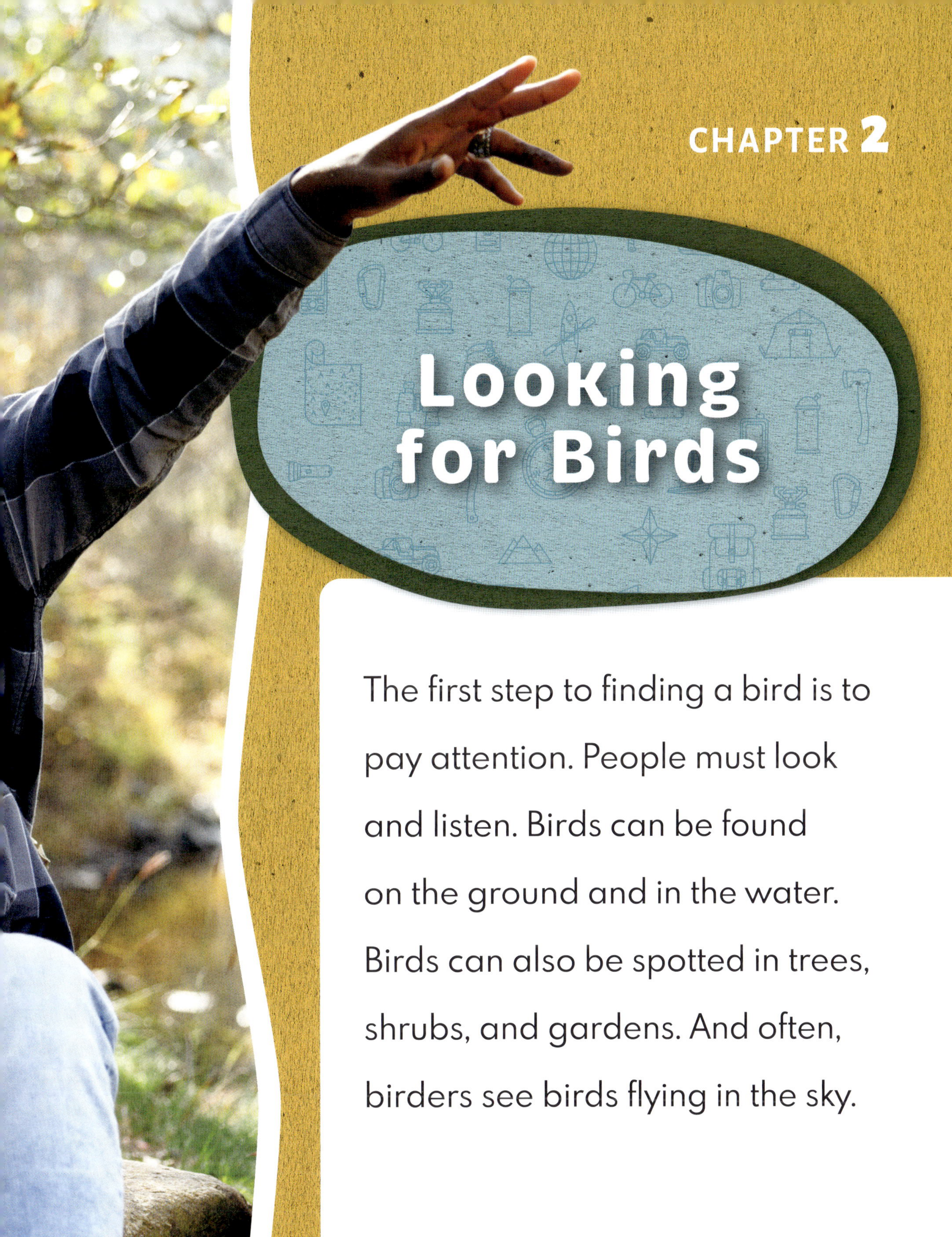

CHAPTER 2

Looking for Birds

The first step to finding a bird is to pay attention. People must look and listen. Birds can be found on the ground and in the water. Birds can also be spotted in trees, shrubs, and gardens. And often, birders see birds flying in the sky.

People can attract birds to homes by putting up bird baths. Some birders visit a park or green space and sit quietly. Shorelines and forest edges are places where two different habitats meet. They are good places to spot birds.

Timing

The time of day affects what types of birds people see. Many birds are active in the early morning. Birders might also hear the dawn chorus. Songbirds such as finches, chickadees, robins, and cardinals sing at this time.

Raptors become active in the late morning. The afternoon is a quiet time for birds. Spotting birds can be more difficult then.

People can set up bird feeders to attract birds.

In the evening, birds become active again. At night, birds may be hard to see, but some are easy to hear. Owls, northern mockingbirds, and whippoorwills are active at night.

Weather affects bird activity. Birds are less active on very hot or very cold days. Right before or after a storm is a good time to

Red-tailed hawks can be found perched on fences and other structures.

spot birds. Birds stay sheltered during storms. Birders should too!

People see different birds throughout the seasons. Many birds **migrate**. In the fall, some birds in cold **climates** migrate south for the winter. In the spring, they return.

Spring is a great time for birding. Birds are building nests and laying eggs. Once the eggs hatch, adult birds are busy finding food for their young through the summer. Depending on location, winter can be a quiet time for birders. However, some trees lose their leaves in the fall. That makes spotting birds much easier.

A Rare Find

Millions of birds migrate every spring and fall. Some make short stops to rest and eat during their journeys. This makes migration a great time to spot birds. Birders may see birds that are not usually in an area.

Field guides include pictures and information about size, habitat, migration, and other details to help identify birds.

A camera with powerful zoom can be helpful for bird-watching.

Bird-Spotting Tools

Patience is an important tool for birders. They might not see birds right away on an outing.

They may need to make several trips to see certain birds.

Many birders carry binoculars for a closer look at birds. A camera helps too. Some birders carry a logbook to record the birds they see. They can use the information to look up the species later.

Wood ducks are among the
birds found near shorelines.

CHAPTER 3

Identifying Birds

Part of the fun of birding is identifying birds. The habitat where a bird is spotted is one clue to identification. Mallards are most often spotted along the water's edge. Cactus wrens are found in desert areas.

The time of day and the season provide more clues to a bird's identity.

Size and shape are other clues used to identify birds. People can compare a bird's size with the size of other birds they are more familiar with. Birders look at the length of a bird's tail and the shape of its beak.

Great Backyard Bird Count

Every February, people around the world participate in the Great Backyard Bird Count. Birders identify and count the birds in their yards or neighborhoods. They share the information and photos online. This helps scientists collect worldwide data on wild birds.

They observe a bird's overall body shape and its wing shape.

Feather colors help identify birds too. This includes looking at patterns, stripes, and spots on different parts of a bird's body. The downy woodpecker has a black-and-white pattern on the body with a broad white stripe down the back. The male has a bright red patch on the back of the head.

Key Parts of a Bird

Birders can study a bird's features to find out what species it is.

A bird's behavior can aid identification. For example, crows and ravens are difficult to tell apart from a distance. However, crows are social. They are usually with a large flock. Ravens are most often spotted alone or with one other raven. Birders also note what a bird is doing, how it moves or flies, and what it eats. They can listen to a bird's call or song to find out which bird it might be.

Resources for Birders

Birders use many resources to identify birds. Some carry field guides. Many parks have booklets or checklists of the birds in that area. Apps can help birders identify birds by picture, call, or description.

There are online bird databases too. Birders can use databases to find birds near them. They can add the birds they see to some databases. Doing so contributes to science. Scientists use the information to learn more about birds' movements and needs. The information helps others to spot and identify birds too. Then even more people can have fun looking for birds!

David Sibley is an American ornithologist. He has written and illustrated many bird guides. In his book for young readers, Sibley says:

> To get started in birding, all you need is curiosity! . . . We should try to disturb all birds as little as possible. Watching from afar is the way to go.

Source: David Allen Sibley. *What It's Like to Be a Bird, Adapted for Young Readers*. Delacorte, 2023.

What's the Big Idea?

Read this quote. What is its main idea? Explain how the main idea is supported by what you've read in this book.

Field Notes

Binoculars and field guide

Logbook

Camera

Bird-Watching Log

Name of bird:
Northern cardinal

Date and time spotted:
May 10, morning

Weather:
Clear

Habitat where spotted:
Shrubs in backyard

Size and body shape:
Similar size as blue jay;
head crest

Color and patterns:
Red with black face

Sketch of bird:

Beak shape:
Thick wedge
shape

Wing shape:
N/A, perching

Tail shape:
Long

Behavior notes:
Singing

A blank Bird-Watching Log is available
at **abdocorelibrary.com.**

Glossary

climates
areas with specific weather patterns

dawn chorus
the collective singing of birds as the sun rises, especially in the spring and summer

habitat
the natural environment where a plant or animal lives

migrate
to move regularly from one place to another

raptors
birds of prey such as eagles, owls, or hawks

talons
sharp claws used for hunting, such as those of a raptor

urban
describing a city

Online Resources

To learn more about birds and bird-watching, visit our free resource websites below.

Visit **abdocorelibrary.com** or scan this QR code for free Common Core resources for teachers and students, including vetted activities, multimedia, and booklinks, for deeper subject comprehension.

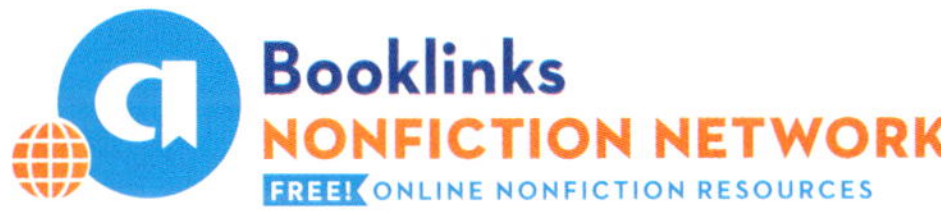

Visit **abdobooklinks.com** or scan this QR code for free additional online weblinks for further learning. These links are routinely monitored and updated to provide the most current information available.

Learn More

Kelly, Christa. *Bird Projects*. Abdo, 2026.

Mayntz, Melissa. *Birds for Kids*. Sourcebooks, 2024.

Sibley, David. *What It's Like to Be a Bird, Adapted for Young Readers*. Delacorte, 2023.

Index

behavior, 12–16, 25
bird traits, 8–9, 22–23, 24, 25

colors, 23

flightless birds, 6

Great Backyard Bird Count, 22

habitats, 7, 11–12, 21

migration, 15, 16

ornithologists, 7, 27

resources, 25–26

seasons, 15–16, 22

time of day, 12–14, 22
tools, 18–19

weather, 14–15

About the Author

Laura Perdew is an author coach, presenter, and former teacher and the author of more than 60 fiction and nonfiction books for kids. She is also a birder! Not only does she have a feeder in her yard, but she also looks for birds whenever she's outside (which is often). She lives in Boulder, Colorado.